AF885496

This Pinterest Workbook and Planner Belongs to:

If found, contact me here:

Phone: ______________________

Email: ______________________

Address ______________________

Dedicated To

YOU and my clients

Published by
GreyChild Communications
Toronto, ON

Pinterest Workbook and Planner / Dwainia Grey
ISBN-13: 978-0994888891

ISBN-10: 0994888899

WHAT IS THIS?

This is the **Pinterest Workbook and Planner** that will help you succeed with Pinterest for your Empowerpreneur business. The book is based on the training in Awesome Nation Engagement; it's a companion book as well as a standalone workbook and planner. The Workbook Section of the book helps you create a Pinterest strategy for the year and clarify your Pinterest goals and tactics (action steps). The Planner Section of the book helps you plan your monthly Pinterest strategy and track your monthly actions and milestones to get a clear picture of your Pinterest Return on Investment (ROI).

By having a plan you leverage your time, reach targets (people and goals), add automation and measure success.

HOW TO USE THIS WORKBOOK

The first part is the Strategy Workbook, which includes worksheets and checklists for you to complete. This helps you develop the Pinterest Marketing Plan and success strategy for the coming months.

1. Objective	9. Pinterest Profile Worksheet
2. Audience	10. Pinterest Boards
3. Style Guide	11. Pinterest Board Ideas
4. Engagement in 15 Minutes	12. Pinterest Group Boards
5. Do's and Don'ts	13. Pinterest Hashtags
6. Planning	14. Getting Started Cheat Sheet
7. Pinterest Pin Ideas	15. Blog Stats
8. 52 Weeks	16. Pinterest Yearly Stats

The second section is the **Pinterest Action Planner**:

1. Monthly Calendar
2. Monthly Success Tracker
3. Monthly Stats
4. Pins
5. Pinterest Campaign Planner
6. To Do
7. Notes

The planner section helps you plan your Pinterest posts and engagement for the next 12 months. Each month includes monthly planning tools as well as metrics trackers. At the end of each month review the month and start planning for the new month. It's very important to complete your success tracker as it helps you to duplicate success.

The downloadable PDF contains 36 pages and allows you to print pages as needed.

PINTEREST TODAY

What is the biggest challenge that you are facing right now with Pinterest?

What do you hope to accomplish?

What have you done so far to get your Pinterest campaign started?

How much time do you currently spend on Pinterest a week?

Are you directing Pinterest followers to your email list?

Are you currently using any of the following tools?

- ☐ Pinterest
- ☐ Linkedin
- ☐ Pinterest
- ☐ YouTube
- ☐ Pinterest
- ☐ Google+
- ☐ Instagram
- ☐ Other sites

Pinterest MARKETING WORKBOOK

Objective

Objective Overall Pinterest objective for the year.

Increase reach
Build your brand
Engage influencers and connectors
Increase customer loyalty
Drive people to events
Improve customer service
Generate leads and sales
Convert leads to sales

Short-term

Goal # 1 –

Deadline

Action Plan

Goal Met ☐ Yes ☐ NO

Goal # 2 –

Deadline

Action Plan

Goal Met ☐ Yes ☐ NO

Goal # 3 –

Deadline

Action Plan

Goal Met ☐ Yes ☐ NO

Long-term

Goal –

Deadline

Action Plan

Goal Met ☐ Yes ☐ NO

Monthly Goal Setter

Set realistic achievable goals for each month.
Goals can be a number of posts or number of new followers to engagement. Make sure it's measurable.

January	February
Goal Met ☐ Yes ☐NO	Goal Met ☐ Yes ☐NO
March	April
Goal Met ☐ Yes ☐NO	Goal Met ☐ Yes ☐NO
May	June
Goal Met ☐ Yes ☐NO	Goal Met ☐ Yes ☐NO
July	August
Goal Met ☐ Yes ☐NO	Goal Met ☐ Yes ☐NO
September	October
Goal Met ☐ Yes ☐NO	Goal Met ☐ Yes ☐NO
November	December
Goal Met ☐ Yes ☐NO	Goal Met ☐ Yes ☐NO

Audience

Your Audience

- ☐ Existing clients
- ☐ Prospective clients

Where they are hanging out:

- ☐ Pinterest
- ☐ Facebook
- ☐ Twitter
- ☐ Instagram
- ☐ Google+
- ☐
- ☐
- ☐

Who are Your Competitors? – How Do They Use Pinterest? – How are You Different?

What Keeps Your Client Up at Night?

How Does Your Product / Service Solve the Problem?

List 3 Successes You Have Had with Clients
Think RESULTS

Audience

What Words or Phrases Do Your Clients Use to Describe the Problem?	What Words or Phrases Do Your Clients Use When They are Looking for the Solution? (KEYWORDS)

Your Avatar

Name (fictitious):
Gender:
Age:
Profession:
Marital and Family Status:
Associations:
Location (city, neighborhood, or postal code):

Style Guide

Pinterest MARKETING

Image Text 1

Font
Size
Style
Color
Hex
RGB
CMYK

Image Text 2

Font
Size
Style
Color
Hex
RGB
CMYK

Watermark Text 1

Font
Size
Style
Color
Hex
RGB
CMYK

Image Sizes

Profile 165 x 165 px

Board Cover 222 x 150 px

Post Template 735 x any length px (Ratio 2:3 or 1:35)

Show placement of graphics, watermark, text alignment, borders etc.

Notes

Separate post templates for blog posts, quotes, promotions, etc?

Create templates using Photoshop, Fireworks, Canva, or Picmonkey.

Voice, tone, abbreviations, spellings and punctuation to use:

Hashtags and descriptive words:

15 Minutes A Day of Engagement

Pinterest MARKETING

	Day 1	Day 2
3-5 Minutes	**Pin, like, and comment on other people's content.**	**Pin, like, and comment on other people's content.**
1-5 Minutes	**Notifications** ☐ Answer Comments (Good and Bad) ☐ Respond to Messages	**Notifications** ☐ Answer Comments (Good and Bad) ☐ Respond to Messages
1-5 Minutes	**Start a Conversation** Message someone	**Make A New Friend** ☐ Influencers ☐ Current, Past and Future Clients ☐ Future Collaborators

AIM FOR A MINIMUM OF 25 REPINS A DAY

Increase Engagement by Integrating Pinterest on Your Website

- ☐ Pinterest Profile buttons
- ☐ Pinterest Widget
- ☐ Custom Pin It button on your website as a reminder to pin and permission
- ☐ Embed Pinterest posts on blog posts

Schedule

- ☐ Schedule other peoples posts using scheduling tools
- ☐ Schedule your blog posts

Pinterest Do's and Don'ts

Pinterest MARKETING

- ☐ Always follow the rules and regulations for Pinterest. Read the Pinterest Page Terms.
- ☐ Do create a social media marketing plan, but adjust your specific tactics as you go. Be flexible and take the time to find out what works and what doesn't work.
- ☐ Do pay attention to social media ethics
- ☐ Don't be disrespectful, offensive, vulgar or use language considered to be inflammatory. Don't be rude or difficult to deal with when engaging with your followers.
- ☐ Do add a relevant link to your pin even when uploading images.
- ☐ Do answer all messages and mentions in a timely manner.
- ☐ Do commit the time and effort to maintain your Pinterest marketing plan.
- ☐ Do create custom image for services and products pages.
- ☐ Do engage with people who have similar interests
- ☐ Do use Pinterest group boards and follow the group board rules.
- ☐ Do ensure every blog post has a custom, branded pinnable image.
- ☐ Do post Pinterest friendly images on blog posts with keyword rich descriptions in alt tags.
- ☐ Do use Rich Pins.
- ☐ Do ensure pins are linked to the right content.
- ☐ Do find the best times to post.
- ☐ Do host and participate in pin parties.
- ☐ Do use video on Pinterest.
- ☐ Do listen to your clients through your Pinterest account and respond promptly and where appropriate.
- ☐ Do mention people and companies where appropriate
- ☐ Do more than one version of your pin. Use different overlay, text image, and descriptions.
- ☐ Do pay attention to the metrics and analytics of your campaign.
- ☐ Do review what pins come from your website (http://pinterest.com/source/**yourwebsite.com**)
- ☐ Do pin other people's content and mention them
- ☐ Do respond to mentions.
- ☐ Do schedule pins.
- ☐ Do search engine optimize (SEO) you pin description with keywords and hashtags. (Pins are indexed by Google)
- ☐ Do share boards and pins on other social media platforms.
- ☐ Do use Promoted Pins.

Pinterest Do's and Don'ts

- ☐ Do support the promotional campaigns of other non-competitive businesses and your followers.
- ☐ Do create and use group boards.
- ☐ Do thank people who pin from your blog where the pin source is your blog.
- ☐ Do unfollow inactive accounts.
- ☐ Do use hashtags.
- ☐ Do use the Pinterest browser extension to make pinning easy.
- ☐ Always use **P.R.O.U.D**. pins. Pretty, Relevant (to your niche or interests), Original, Useful, Descriptive.
- ☐ Do prepare to deal with how online users change, alter or use your brand's message. Have a plan for both good and bad customer feedback.
- ☐ Don't just post your own content
- ☐ Don't hijack others pins.
- ☐ Don't forget to add attribution when it's not your content. Use the @ tag in description – gives credit and notifies pinner.
- ☐ Don't lie to your audience or hide the fact that you are advertising to them. Always be transparent with your intentions
- ☐ Don't overdo it when promoting your business. You want to use Pinterest to build relationships, not overwhelm users with ads.
- ☐ Don't overload Pinterest group boards.
- ☐ Don't overuse hashtags
- ☐ Don't spam!

Day-to-Day Management

How many times a week will you post on Pinterest?
Suggested number of times a week to post: min 10 posts a day

What days and times will you post?

How far ahead do you want to plan content?

How often will you promote your own content (blog posts, events, products and services) versus other people's content?

What type of content are you going to share? Review the Post Idea Sheet. What you share needs to bring value - always think "What's in it for me?" Try for a combination of educating, and engaging. You are aiming to get them interested in you, your brand, and your business.

Who will create content? Images / Video / Copy

Who will post content?

Who will manage your Pinterest campaigns?

Who will track, monitor, and report?

Number of people to follow each week:

Planning

Do you want to assign posts to certain days a week? Throwback Thursday, Follow Friday, or make up your own

	Themed Post	Create Content	Publish Content
Monday			
Tuesday			
Wednesday			
Thursday			
Friday			
Saturday			
Sunday			

Resources

- ☐ Experienced Writer
- ☐ Professional Photos / Photo shoot
- ☐ Professional Videos / Video shoot
- ☐ Branded Graphics

Pinterest Policy

Develop your Pinterest Policy.
Read the Do's and Don'ts of Pinterest. What are the policies you will have for your Empowerpreneur business?

- Rules of engagement
- How to handle customer service
- What to say and what not to say
- Workflow / Schedule
- How to handle negative feedback /criticism
    - Clients, media or competitors

Budget

Startup and launch budget
Campaign budgets
Ongoing management budget
- Advertising
- Design
- Tools (Canva, Pic Monkey, Hootsuite, Buffer, etc)

Metrics

Review your online metrics on a weekly and/or monthly basis. Use Google Analytics in conjunction with bitly, and the Pinterest Insights to track and monitor your success. Also use Buffer and Hootsuite reporting tools.

Learn more about your return on investment (ROI – time and money) as well as which posts brings the most traffic, engagement and conversion.

Take time to complete the Blog Stats, Monthly Success Tracker and The Monthly and Yearly Social Media Stats.

Va Va VooM ™

Va Va VooM ™ (Content Marketing Ratio)

Value – 40% - Tips, tutorials, and instructional useful and helpful posts

List 3 topics that you can post about that will add value

Visual – 45% - Make use of images and videos

List 3 ways you can use images / videos in social media

Voice – 5% - Show your personality – personal posts about you, showing your life, and a behind the scenes view

List 3 posts that will show your personality

Marketing – 10% - Promotional posts to sell and promote your products and services

List 3 products / services you want to sell / promote via social media

Content Ideas for Pinterest

1	**Valuable and Useful Information**	2	**Blog Posts** Ensure every blog has a branded, pinnable image.	3	**Influencers' Posts**	4	**Personal Posts** - your life - lifestyle - personal interests
5	**Seasonal** Seasonal products and promotions.	6	**Funny** Humorous posts	7	**Pinterest Exclusives** Pinterest only events, products, and promotions.	8	**Events, Workshops and Seminars** Share online and offline events you are hosting or attending.
9	**Your Work** Post updates about your work.	10	**Testimonials** Post client testimonials and tag them.	11	**Business News** Updates about your business and industry.	12	**Gift Ideas** Pin gift ideas for your niche.
13	**Quotes** Post quotes that will motivate and inspire your audience.	14	**Products / Services** Links and, images to your products and services.	15	**Video / Photos** Pictures and videos of your products and customers using your products.	16	**Lifestyle** Pin your lifestyle and your niches lifestyle.
17	**Promotions** Promote your products, services, sales, and coupons. Use contests, giveaways, and sweepstakes.	18	**Contests** Pinterest exclusive contests.	19	**Sales** Soft Sell – Link to tips, resources, freebies and printables.	20	**Sales** Hard Sell – Link to products with product description and price.

52 Weeks

Pinterest MARKETING

Plan out 52 weeks of Tips, Quotes, etc
52 Weeks of ___________________________

1		27	
2		28	
3		29	
4		30	
5		31	
6		32	
7		33	
8		34	
9		35	
10		36	
11		37	
12		38	
13		39	
14		40	
15		41	
16		42	
17		43	
18		44	
19		45	
20		46	
21		47	
22		48	
23		49	
24		50	
25		51	
26		52	

Pinterest Profile

- ☐ Pinterest business account
- ☐ Business Name
- ☐ Professional Profile Image or logo
- ☐ About you – Branded, search optimized profile (160 Characters)
- ☐ Location
- ☐ Website URL

Optimized Bio

Notes

Board Ideas for Pinterest

1	**Your Blog Post**	2	**Any Media Coverage**	3	**Contact Info and Social Media Profiles**	4	**Behind-the-Scenes** - Your Office - Your Team - You Working - Your Story
5	**Products and Services**	6	**Events** - Attending - Hosting - Past and Upcoming	7	**Resources for You Niche and Clients**	8	**Products Your Recommend**
9	**Inspirational Quotes**	10	**People and Influencers Who Inspire You**	11	**Things that Inspire Your Work**	12	**Books, Magazines, and Websites Worth Reading**
13	**How to ...** Posts and videos	14	**Niche Infographics**	15	**Gift Ideas**	16	**Lifestyle of Your Clients**
17	**Group Board for Clients to Contribute**	18	**Client Logos**	19	**Testimonials and Case Studies**	20	**Before and After**

Pinterest Boards

Pinterest Boards	Description	Contents

Notes

Hashtags

#Hashtags to Use	✓

Use hashtags. List popular hashtags for your preferred client, industry, and niche. Create hashtags for your business, and products and services.

Getting Started Cheat Sheet

Pinterest MARKETING

Branding

- ☐ I have a clear description of who my target audience is.
- ☐ My preferred client is using Pinterest.
- ☐ I have included a professional photo or logo on my Pinterest profile?
- ☐ My Pinterest name is easy to find, follow, and connect with.
  - ☐ It's my name, business name, brand name or based on an SEO keyword.
  - ☐ It's the same as my other social media profile names for consistency
- ☐ I have a completed Pinterest Business Account.
- ☐ Pinterest "About You" includes keywords and reflects my voice and brand.
- ☐ I have set up Rich Pins.
- ☐ I know what personality/ brand message and image I want to communicate.
- ☐ I have included a professional email address - @yourwebsite.com
- ☐ I have included my business location (where applicable - at least put country)
- ☐ I link to other social media profiles (where applicable)

Planning

- ☐ I know my Pinterest objective
- ☐ I have defined my Pinterest marketing goals and know how I will track them.
- ☐ I've created systems to test and track my social media marketing goals and tactics.
- ☐ I have a *Social Media Marketing Plan* that I use to help guide my online marketing and I've integrated my Pinterest marketing tactics into my overall social media marketing strategies.
- ☐ I've use relevant dashboards and automation tools such as Tailwind for Hootsuite to optimize my time.
- ☐ I've documented the systems and tools I use, so it can be easily delegated.
- ☐ I use Pinterest Analytics to create targeted posts and know the best day and time for engagement
- ☐ I use Pinterest Advertising
- ☐ I have a (monthly/ weekly / daily) posting schedule for Pinterest
- ☐ I have a (monthly/ weekly/ daily) Pinterest engagement schedule
  - ☐ Pin awesome content
  - ☐ Respond to all messages and comments
  - ☐ Mention people when you pin their content direct from their website
  - ☐ Follow new people
- ☐ I have a strategy to capture leads from Pinterest and to get followers to buy

Getting Started Cheat Sheet

Pinterest MARKETING

Content

- ☐ I have developed a system to find valuable content to share on Pinterest
- ☐ I make sure I share a good mix of content (*Va Va VooM* – Value, Voice, Visual and Marketing)
- ☐ I use a Call To Action in posts
- ☐ I'm creating specific promotions and offers for my Pinterest audience - *EXCLUSIVE.*
- ☐ I use an editorial calendar to layout content for my blog, and Pinterest posts.
- ☐ I schedule blog posts as they are published, a week later, and a month later.
- ☐ I create a schedule to promote old blog posts.
- ☐ I use Pinterest Analytics to find the optimal day and time to post content for maximum engagement
- ☐ I follow the top blogs in my industry to stay on top of trends.
- ☐ I create specific content to share on Pinterest
- ☐ I always check for grammar and spelling

Pinterest Tools

- ☐ Pinterest Analytics
- ☐ Hootsuite
- ☐ Buffer
- ☐ Canva
- ☐ Picmonkey
- ☐ Pixlr
- ☐ Ahology
- ☐ Viraltag
- ☐ BoardBooster
- ☐ Tailwind
- ☐ Photoshop

Blog Stats

Pinterest MARKETING

	Date	Pinterest	Facebook	Google+	Twitter	Instagram	Blog Visits
1							
2							
3							
4							
5							
6							
7							
8							
9							
10							
11							
12							
13							
14							
15							
16							
17							
18							
19							
20							
21							
22							
23							
24							
25							
26							
27							
28							
29							
30							
31							
32							
33							
34							
35							
36							
37							
38							
39							
40							
41							
42							
43							
44							
45							
46							
47							
48							
49							
50							
51							
52							

Yearly Stats

Year	Total Followers		# of Retweets		# of Posts		# of Favourites		# of Comments		# of Clicks to Website	
	Goal	Actual	Goal	Actual	Goal	Actual	Goal	Actual	Goal	Actual	Goal	Actual
January												
February												
March												
April												
May												
June												
July												
August												
September												
October												
November												
December												
Yearly Total												

Pinterest MARKETING PLANNER

Month

SUNDAY	MONDAY	TUESDAY	WEDNESDAY	THURSDAY	FRIDAY	SATURDAY

Notes

Acknowledge and Celebrate Your Success

Month:

Total Followers

Post with most engagement (Pins, Likes, and Comments) on Pinterest

---

Post with most clicks

Blog post with most traffic from Pinterest

This month, I learned

A record I broke this month

My celebration this month

Next month, I plan to do the same

Next month, I plan to try (new)

Monthly Stats

GOAL:

Total Followers	New Followers	# of Posts	# of Pins	# of Likes	# of Comments	# of Mentions	# of Clicks	# of Clicks to Website

EMAIL SUBSCRIBERS FROM PINTEREST	

ENGAGEMENT

Post with most pins	
Post with most likes	
Post with most comments	
Post with most clicks	

PINTEREST ADS

Spend $		Results	

Pins

Pins	Date	Time	✓

Product / Service Campaign

Campaign	
Description	
Product / Service Newsletter Contest / Giveaway	
Start	End
Objective	
Target Audience	
Budget$ / Cost$ / Return$	
Landing Page	
Tracking Link	
Days and Time	
Winner / Date Notified	

Image

- ☐ Blog Post Announcement
- ☐ Blog Post Follow-up
- ☐ Autoresponder Setup
- ☐ Ad Campaign
  - ○ Budget$
  - ○ Cost$
  - ○ Return$
  - ○ Click Thru Rate
  - ○ CPC (Cost per Click)
- ☐ Conversion Rate
- ☐ Hashtag
- ☐ Coupon Code (if applicable)

Advertising Campaign

Campaign	
Boost / Ad	
Description	
Start	End
Objective	
Target Audience	
Budget$ / Cost Per Day$	
Landing Page	
Tracking Link	

Text

Demographic

Image

To Do

Pinterest MARKETING

	Priority	Completed

Notes

Editorial Calendar

Pinterest MARKETING

Month

SUNDAY	MONDAY	TUESDAY	WEDNESDAY	THURSDAY	FRIDAY	SATURDAY

Notes

Success Tracker

Acknowledge and Celebrate Your Success

Month:

Total Followers

Post with most engagement (Pins, Likes, and Comments) on Pinterest

---

Post with most clicks

Blog post with most traffic from Pinterest

This month, I learned

A record I broke this month

My celebration this month

Next month, I plan to do the same

Next month, I plan to try (new)

Monthly Stats

GOAL:

Total Followers	New Followers	# of Posts	# of Pins	# of Likes	# of Comments	# of Mentions	# of Clicks	# of Clicks to Website

EMAIL SUBSCRIBERS FROM PINTEREST	
ENGAGEMENT	
Post with most pins	
Post with most likes	
Post with most comments	
Post with most clicks	

PINTEREST ADS			
Spend $		Results	

Pins	Date	Time	✓

Product / Service Campaign

Campaign	
Description	
Product / Service Newsletter Contest / Giveaway	
Start	End
Objective	
Target Audience	
Budget$ / Cost$ / Return$	
Landing Page	
Tracking Link	
Days and Time	
Winner / Date Notified	

Image

- ☐ Blog Post Announcement
- ☐ Blog Post Follow-up
- ☐ Autoresponder Setup
- ☐ Ad Campaign
  - Budget$
  - Cost$
  - Return$
  - Click Thru Rate
  - CPC (Cost per Click)
- ☐ Conversion Rate
- ☐ Hashtag
- ☐ Coupon Code (if applicable)

Advertising Campaign

Campaign	
Boost / Ad	
Description	
Start	End
Objective	
Target Audience	
Budget$ / Cost Per Day$	
Landing Page	
Tracking Link	

Text

Demographic

Image

To Do

	Priority	Completed

Notes

Month

SUNDAY	MONDAY	TUESDAY	WEDNESDAY	THURSDAY	FRIDAY	SATURDAY

Notes

Acknowledge and Celebrate Your Success

Month:

Total Followers

Post with most engagement (Pins, Likes, and Comments) on Pinterest

Post with most clicks

Blog post with most traffic from Pinterest

This month, I learned

A record I broke this month

My celebration this month

Next month, I plan to do the same

Next month, I plan to try (new)

Monthly Stats

GOAL:

Total Followers	New Followers	# of Posts	# of Pins	# of Likes	# of Comments	# of Mentions	# of Clicks	# of Clicks to Website

EMAIL SUBSCRIBERS FROM PINTEREST	
ENGAGEMENT	
Post with most pins	
Post with most likes	
Post with most comments	
Post with most clicks	
PINTEREST ADS	

Spend $		Results	

Pins	Date	Time	✓

Product / Service Campaign

Campaign	
Description	
Product / Service Newsletter Contest / Giveaway	
Start	End
Objective	
Target Audience	
Budget$ / Cost$ / Return$	
Landing Page	
Tracking Link	
Days and Time	
Winner / Date Notified	

Image

- ☐ Blog Post Announcement
- ☐ Blog Post Follow-up
- ☐ Autoresponder Setup
- ☐ Ad Campaign
  - Budget$
  - Cost$
  - Return$
  - Click Thru Rate
  - CPC (Cost per Click)
- ☐ Conversion Rate
- ☐ Hashtag
- ☐ Coupon Code (if applicable)

Advertising Campaign

Campaign	
Boost / Ad	
Description	
Start	End
Objective	
Target Audience	
Budget$ / Cost Per Day$	
Landing Page	
Tracking Link	

Text

Demographic

Image

	Priority	Completed

Notes

Month

SUNDAY	MONDAY	TUESDAY	WEDNESDAY	THURSDAY	FRIDAY	SATURDAY

Notes

Acknowledge and Celebrate Your Success

Month:

Total Followers

Post with most engagement (Pins, Likes, and Comments) on Pinterest

---

Post with most clicks

Blog post with most traffic from Pinterest

This month, I learned

A record I broke this month

My celebration this month

Next month, I plan to do the same

Next month, I plan to try (new)

Monthly Stats

GOAL:

Total Followers	New Followers	# of Posts	# of Pins	# of Likes	# of Comments	# of Mentions	# of Clicks	# of Clicks to Website

EMAIL SUBSCRIBERS FROM PINTEREST	
ENGAGEMENT	
Post with most pins	
Post with most likes	
Post with most comments	
Post with most clicks	

PINTEREST ADS			
Spend $		Results	

Pins	Date	Time	✓

Product / Service Campaign

Campaign	
Description	
Product / Service Newsletter Contest / Giveaway	
Start	End
Objective	
Target Audience	
Budget$ / Cost$ / Return$	
Landing Page	
Tracking Link	
Days and Time	
Winner / Date Notified	

Image

- ☐ Blog Post Announcement
- ☐ Blog Post Follow-up
- ☐ Autoresponder Setup
- ☐ Ad Campaign
  - Budget$
  - Cost$
  - Return$
  - Click Thru Rate
  - CPC (Cost per Click)
- ☐ Conversion Rate
- ☐ Hashtag
- ☐ Coupon Code (if applicable)

Advertising Campaign

Campaign	
Boost / Ad	
Description	
Start	End
Objective	
Target Audience	
Budget$ / Cost Per Day$	
Landing Page	
Tracking Link	

Text

Demographic

Image

	Priority	Completed

Notes

Month

SUNDAY	MONDAY	TUESDAY	WEDNESDAY	THURSDAY	FRIDAY	SATURDAY

Notes

Acknowledge and Celebrate Your Success

Month:

Total Followers

Post with most engagement (Pins, Likes, and Comments) on Pinterest

---

Post with most clicks

Blog post with most traffic from Pinterest

This month, I learned

A record I broke this month

My celebration this month

Next month, I plan to do the same

Next month, I plan to try (new)

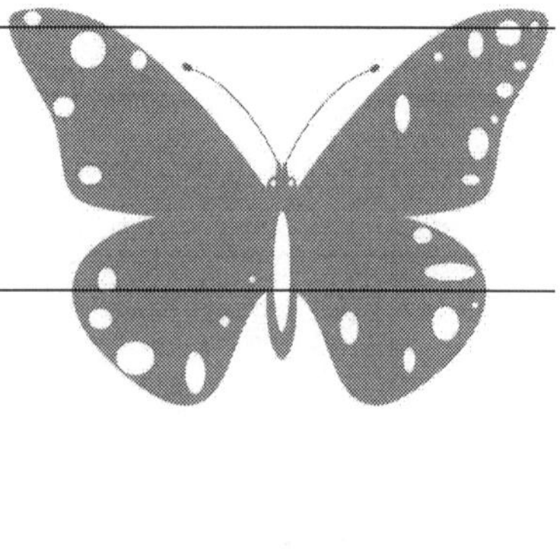

Monthly Stats

GOAL:

Total Followers	New Followers	# of Posts	# of Pins	# of Likes	# of Comments	# of Mentions	# of Clicks	# of Clicks to Website

EMAIL SUBSCRIBERS FROM PINTEREST	
ENGAGEMENT	
Post with most pins	
Post with most likes	
Post with most comments	
Post with most clicks	
PINTEREST ADS	

Spend $		Results	

Pins	Date	Time	✓

Product / Service Campaign

Campaign	
Description	
Product / Service Newsletter Contest / Giveaway	
Start	End
Objective	
Target Audience	
Budget$ / Cost$ / Return$	
Landing Page	
Tracking Link	
Days and Time	
Winner / Date Notified	

Image

- ☐ Blog Post Announcement
- ☐ Blog Post Follow-up
- ☐ Autoresponder Setup
- ☐ Ad Campaign
  - Budget$
  - Cost$
  - Return$
  - Click Thru Rate
  - CPC (Cost per Click)
- ☐ Conversion Rate
- ☐ Hashtag
- ☐ Coupon Code (if applicable)

Advertising Campaign

Campaign	
Boost / Ad	
Description	
Start	End
Objective	
Target Audience	
Budget$ / Cost Per Day$	
Landing Page	
Tracking Link	

Text	Demographic

Image

	Priority	Completed

Editorial Calendar

Pinterest MARKETING

Month

SUNDAY	MONDAY	TUESDAY	WEDNESDAY	THURSDAY	FRIDAY	SATURDAY

Notes

Acknowledge and Celebrate Your Success

Month:

Total Followers

Post with most engagement (Pins, Likes, and Comments) on Pinterest

---

Post with most clicks

Blog post with most traffic from Pinterest

This month, I learned

A record I broke this month

My celebration this month

Next month, I plan to do the same

Next month, I plan to try (new)

Monthly Stats

GOAL:

Total Followers	New Followers	# of Posts	# of Pins	# of Likes	# of Comments	# of Mentions	# of Clicks	# of Clicks to Website

EMAIL SUBSCRIBERS FROM PINTEREST	
ENGAGEMENT	
Post with most pins	
Post with most likes	
Post with most comments	
Post with most clicks	

PINTEREST ADS

Spenc $		Results	

Pins	Date	Time	✓

Campaign Manager

Pinterest MARKETING

Product / Service Campaign

Campaign	
Description	
Product / Service Newsletter Contest / Giveaway	
Start	End
Objective	
Target Audience	
Budget$ / Cost$ / Return$	
Landing Page	
Tracking Link	
Days and Time	
Winner / Date Notified	

Image

- ☐ Blog Post Announcement
- ☐ Blog Post Follow-up
- ☐ Autoresponder Setup
- ☐ Ad Campaign
  - Budget$
  - Cost$
  - Return$
  - Click Thru Rate
  - CPC (Cost per Click)
- ☐ Conversion Rate
- ☐ Hashtag
- ☐ Coupon Code (if applicable)

Advertising Campaign

Campaign	
Boost / Ad	
Description	
Start	End
Objective	
Target Audience	
Budget$ / Cost Per Day$	
Landing Page	
Tracking Link	

Text

Demographic

Image

To Do

	Priority	Completed

Editorial Calendar

Pinterest MARKETING

Month

SUNDAY	MONDAY	TUESDAY	WEDNESDAY	THURSDAY	FRIDAY	SATURDAY

Notes

Acknowledge and Celebrate Your Success

Month:

Total Followers

Post with most engagement (Pins, Likes, and Comments) on Pinterest

---

Post with most clicks

Blog post with most traffic from Pinterest

This month, I learned

A record I broke this month

My celebration this month

Next month, I plan to do the same

Next month, I plan to try (new)

Monthly Stats

GOAL:

Total Followers	New Followers	# of Posts	# of Pins	# of Likes	# of Comments	# of Mentions	# of Clicks	# of Clicks to Website

EMAIL SUBSCRIBERS FROM PINTEREST	
ENGAGEMENT	
Post with most pins	
Post with most likes	
Post with most comments	
Post with most clicks	
PINTEREST ADS	

Spend $		Results	

Pins	Date	Time	✓

Product / Service Campaign

Campaign	
Description	
Product / Service Newsletter Contest / Giveaway	
Start	End
Objective	
Target Audience	
Budget$ / Cost$ / Return$	
Landing Page	
Tracking Link	
Days and Time	
Winner / Date Notified	

Image

- ☐ Blog Post Announcement
- ☐ Blog Post Follow-up
- ☐ Autoresponder Setup
- ☐ Ad Campaign
  - Budget$
  - Cost$
  - Return$
  - Click Thru Rate
  - CPC (Cost per Click)
- ☐ Conversion Rate
- ☐ Hashtag
- ☐ Coupon Code (if applicable)

Advertising Campaign

Campaign	
Boost / Ad	
Description	
Start	End
Objective	
Target Audience	
Budget$ / Cost Per Day$	
Landing Page	
Tracking Link	

Text

Demographic

Image

To Do

	Priority	Completed

Month

SUNDAY	MONDAY	TUESDAY	WEDNESDAY	THURSDAY	FRIDAY	SATURDAY

Notes

Acknowledge and Celebrate Your Success

Month:

Total Followers

Post with most engagement (Pins, Likes, and Comments) on Pinterest

---

Post with most clicks

Blog post with most traffic from Pinterest

This month, I learned

A record I broke this month

My celebration this month

Next month, I plan to do the same

Next month, I plan to try (new)

Monthly Stats

GOAL:

Total Followers	New Followers	# of Posts	# of Pins	# of Likes	# of Comments	# of Mentions	# of Clicks	# of Clicks to Website

EMAIL SUBSCRIBERS FROM PINTEREST	
ENGAGEMENT	
Post with most pins	
Post with most likes	
Post with most comments	
Post with most clicks	
PINTEREST ADS	

Spend $		Results	

Pins	Date	Time	✓

Campaign Manager

Pinterest MARKETING

Product / Service Campaign

Campaign	
Description	
Product / Service Newsletter Contest / Giveaway	
Start	End
Objective	
Target Audience	
Budget$ / Cost$ / Return$	
Landing Page	
Tracking Link	
Days and Time	
Winner / Date Notified	

Image

- ☐ Blog Post Announcement
- ☐ Blog Post Follow-up
- ☐ Autoresponder Setup
- ☐ Ad Campaign
  - Budget$
  - Cost$
  - Return$
  - Click Thru Rate
  - CPC (Cost per Click)
- ☐ Conversion Rate
- ☐ Hashtag
- ☐ Coupon Code (if applicable)

Advertising Campaign

Campaign	
Boost / Ad	
Description	
Start	End
Objective	
Target Audience	
Budget$ / Cost Per Day$	
Landing Page	
Tracking Link	

Text

Demographic

Image

To Do

Pinterest MARKETING

	Priority	Completed

Notes

Editorial Calendar

Month

SUNDAY	MONDAY	TUESDAY	WEDNESDAY	THURSDAY	FRIDAY	SATURDAY

Notes

Acknowledge and Celebrate Your Success

Month:

Total Followers

Post with most engagement (Pins, Likes, and Comments) on Pinterest

---

Post with most clicks

Blog post with most traffic from Pinterest

This month, I learned

A record I broke this month

My celebration this month

Next month, I plan to do the same

Next month, I plan to try (new)

Monthly Stats

GOAL:

Total Followers	New Followers	# of Posts	# of Pins	# of Likes	# of Comments	# of Mentions	# of Clicks	# of Clicks to Website

EMAIL SUBSCRIBERS FROM PINTEREST	

ENGAGEMENT

Post with most pins	
Post with most likes	
Post with most comments	
Post with most clicks	

PINTEREST ADS

Spend $		Results	

Pins	Date	Time	✓

Product / Service Campaign

Campaign	
Description	
Product / Service Newsletter Contest / Giveaway	
Start	End
Objective	
Target Audience	
Budget$ / Cost$ / Return$	
Landing Page	
Tracking Link	
Days and Time	
Winner / Date Notified	

Image

- ☐ Blog Post Announcement
- ☐ Blog Post Follow-up
- ☐ Autoresponder Setup
- ☐ Ad Campaign
  - Budget$
  - Cost$
  - Return$
  - Click Thru Rate
  - CPC (Cost per Click)
- ☐ Conversion Rate
- ☐ Hashtag
- ☐ Coupon Code (if applicable)

Advertising Campaign

Campaign	
Boost / Ad	
Description	
Start	End
Objective	
Target Audience	
Budget$ / Cost Per Day$	
Landing Page	
Tracking Link	

Text

Demographic

Image

To Do

	Priority	Completed

Notes

Month

SUNDAY	MONDAY	TUESDAY	WEDNESDAY	THURSDAY	FRIDAY	SATURDAY

Notes

Acknowledge and Celebrate Your Success

Month:

Total Followers

Post with most engagement (Pins, Likes, and Comments) on Pinterest

---

Post with most clicks

Blog post with most traffic from Pinterest

This month, I learned

A record I broke this month

My celebration this month

Next month, I plan to do the same

Next month, I plan to try (new)

Monthly Stats

GOAL:

Total Followers	New Followers	# of Posts	# of Pins	# of Likes	# of Comments	# of Mentions	# of Clicks	# of Clicks to Website

EMAIL SUBSCRIBERS FROM PINTEREST	
ENGAGEMENT	
Post with most pins	
Post with most likes	
Post with most comments	
Post with most clicks	

PINTEREST ADS

Spend $		Results	

Pins	Date	Time	✓

Product / Service Campaign

Campaign	
Description	
Product / Service Newsletter Contest / Giveaway	
Start	End
Objective	
Target Audience	
Budget$ / Cost$ / Return$	
Landing Page	
Tracking Link	
Days and Time	
Winner / Date Notified	

Image

- ☐ Blog Post Announcement
- ☐ Blog Post Follow-up
- ☐ Autoresponder Setup
- ☐ Ad Campaign
  - Budget$
  - Cost$
  - Return$
  - Click Thru Rate
  - CPC (Cost per Click)
- ☐ Conversion Rate
- ☐ Hashtag
- ☐ Coupon Code (if applicable)

Advertising Campaign

Campaign	
Boost / Ad	
Description	
Start	End
Objective	
Target Audience	
Budget$ / Cost Per Day$	
Landing Page	
Tracking Link	

Text

Demographic

Image

To Do

Pinterest MARKETING

	Priority	Completed

Editorial Calendar

Pinterest MARKETING

Month

SUNDAY	MONDAY	TUESDAY	WEDNESDAY	THURSDAY	FRIDAY	SATURDAY

Notes

Acknowledge and Celebrate Your Success

Month:

Total Followers

Post with most engagement (Pins, Likes, and Comments) on Pinterest

---

Post with most clicks

Blog post with most traffic from Pinterest

This month, I learned

A record I broke this month

My celebration this month

Next month, I plan to do the same

Next month, I plan to try (new)

Monthly Stats

GOAL:

Total Followers	New Followers	# of Posts	# of Pins	# of Likes	# of Comments	# of Mentions	# of Clicks	# of Clicks to Website

EMAIL SUBSCRIBERS FROM PINTEREST	
ENGAGEMENT	
Post with most pins	
Post with most likes	
Post with most comments	
Post with most clicks	

PINTEREST ADS			
Spend $		Results	

Pins	Date	Time	✓

Product / Service Campaign

Campaign	
Description	
Product / Service Newsletter Contest / Giveaway	
Start	End
Objective	
Target Audience	
Budget$ / Cost$ / Return$	
Landing Page	
Tracking Link	
Days and Time	
Winner / Date Notified	

Image

- ☐ Blog Post Announcement
- ☐ Blog Post Follow-up
- ☐ Autoresponder Setup
- ☐ Ad Campaign
  - Budget$
  - Cost$
  - Return$
  - Click Thru Rate
  - CPC (Cost per Click)
- ☐ Conversion Rate
- ☐ Hashtag
- ☐ Coupon Code (if applicable)

Advertising Campaign

Campaign	
Boost / Ad	
Description	
Start	End
Objective	
Target Audience	
Budget$ / Cost Per Day$	
Landing Page	
Tracking Link	

Text	Demographic

Image

	Priority	Completed

Notes

Editorial Calendar

Pinterest MARKETING

Month

SUNDAY	MONDAY	TUESDAY	WEDNESDAY	THURSDAY	FRIDAY	SATURDAY

Notes

Acknowledge and Celebrate Your Success

Month:

Total Followers

Post with most engagement (Pins, Likes, and Comments) on Pinterest

Post with most clicks

Blog post with most traffic from Pinterest

This month, I learned

A record I broke this month

My celebration this month

Next month, I plan to do the same

Next month, I plan to try (new)

Monthly Stats

GOAL:

Total Followers	New Followers	# of Posts	# of Pins	# of Likes	# of Comments	# of Mentions	# of Clicks	# of Clicks to Website

EMAIL SUBSCRIBERS FROM PINTEREST	

ENGAGEMENT	
Post with most pins	
Post with most likes	
Post with most comments	
Post with most clicks	

PINTEREST ADS			
Spend $		Results	

Pins	Date	Time	✓

Product / Service Campaign

Campaign	
Description	
Product / Service Newsletter Contest / Giveaway	
Start	End
Objective	
Target Audience	
Budget$ / Cost$ / Return$	
Landing Page	
Tracking Link	
Days and Time	
Winner / Date Notified	

Image

- ☐ Blog Post Announcement
- ☐ Blog Post Follow-up
- ☐ Autoresponder Setup
- ☐ Ad Campaign
  - Budget$
  - Cost$
  - Return$
  - Click Thru Rate
  - CPC (Cost per Click)
- ☐ Conversion Rate
- ☐ Hashtag
- ☐ Coupon Code (if applicable)

Advertising Campaign

Campaign	
Boost / Ad	
Description	
Start	End
Objective	
Target Audience	
Budget$ / Cost Per Day$	
Landing Page	
Tracking Link	

Text

Demographic

Image

To Do

	Priority	Completed

HOPE YOU ENJOYED USING
YOUR PINTEREST WORKBOOK AND PLANNER

GET YOUR FREE WEEKLY PINTEREST PLANNER!
http://bit.ly/pinterestweekly

PLEASE LEAVE A REVIEW ON AMAZON

BE SURE TO GRAB YOUR COPIES
- Social Media Marketing Workbook -
- Social Media Marketing Planner -
- Google+ Workbook and Planner -
- LinkedIn Workbook and Planner -
- Facebook Workbook and Planner -
- Twitter Workbook and Planner -
- Instagram Workbook and Planner -

ALSO LOOK OUT FOR
Authentic Marketing – The Three E's of Online Marketing: Ethical, Effortless, Engaging
Social Media Marketing: How to Master Engagement in 15 Minutes a Day.

Connect with Dwainia Grey on LinkedIn, Google+, Facebook, Twitter, Pinterest and Instagram
dwainiagrey.me

Made in the USA
Monee, IL
05 November 2026

67996166R00074